BERWI
BEYOND
PICTURES FROM THE PAST
Jim Walker

ISBN 978-0-9552109-4-5

Published by Blackhall Press in 2011
Telephone 01289 307553
© Jim Walker
www.jim-walker.org.uk

The author asserts his moral right to be
identified as the author of this work.

Printed and bound in Great Britain by
Martins the Printers Limited, Sea View Works,
Spittal, Berwick-upon-Tweed
www.martins-the-printers.com

Design www.simprimstudio.com
Set in Today 8.5 / 10.5

Acknowledgements

For the production of this, my eighth book on Berwick, I have been greatly indebted to the following for help given: -

Linda Bankier, Borough archivist and her staff
Alan Burn
Bob Craig
Clifford H Crook
Ian and Sandra Shiel Dods
Joan Elder
Bobby Johnson
John Kay
Maureen Lyall
Maxi and Sonia McPhillips
Cynthia Mann
Hazel Page
John Pinkerton
Mrs E Rathbone
Mrs E Robertson
Mrs E Short
Ian B Smith, Photo Centre

Also my heartfelt thanks to my wife Connie for her continued support, and a special thank you to my niece Sheila Scott, for one again coping magnificently with the transcribing of all the images and script.

My grateful thanks to all
Jim Walker

Foreword

Shakespeare's play, *Richard III*, has the young Prince of Wales asking, "is it upon record, or else reported successively from age to age?"

Being assured it was on record the Prince said, even it were not reported, he thought the truth "should live from age to age and retailed to all posterity".

And so this book attempts to portray the truth about an age that has gone, by showing scenes of the time at the beginning of the 20th century, that will never be repeated, but deserve to be "retailed to all posterity".

For this to be achieved I have been greatly indebted to two gentlemen, John S Pirie and Anthony T Brown and their respective grandfathers who were accomplished photographers, taking pictures in Berwick in the Edwardian era.

John Pirie's grandfather, Joseph Hunt Thompson, was the son of Ralph Thompson, founder of Thompsons Bakers and Confectioners, Bridge Street, Berwick. Joseph was a meticulous and knowledgeable photographer, absorbed in the history of Berwick. With a magic lantern and glass slides, he gave lectures to appreciative audiences, not only in Berwick and Glasgow (where he settled), but to societies throughout the land.

All Joseph H Thompson's lecture notes and photographic glass plates and lantern slides survive today, thanks to John S Pirie's careful custodianship over many years.

Anthony T Brown's grandfather, Tom Brown, served an apprenticeship with Mr R Atkinson, Dentist, Berwick (corner of Church Street and The Parade), subsequently moving to Middlesbrough, where his son Tom Brown Jnr and grandson Dr. Anthony T Brown all practised as dentists.

The first Tom Brown, photographed scenes in Berwick when on holiday from Middlesbrough, and produced postcards which were sold by his Mother, Ann, in her shop at 66 Church Street, Berwick. The shop was subsequently taken over by Tom's brother Willie, and then by Ann's grandson Thomas James, who retired in 1968 and who is still remembered by Berwickers today.

Dr Anthony T Brown has published a most informative book about the life of his grandfather, which includes photographs of the medals he won, while a member of the Cleveland Camera Club.

Of the photographs in this book, nineteen are by Tom Brown, 53 are by Joseph H Thompson and the rest are from my own archives.

The twentieth century calls us back
so let us start our photographic journey
through Berwick and Beyond.

A new age dawns for the Berwick fire brigade.

In February 1903, Berwick's chief constable made a request to the local Sanitary Authority for a new steam fire engine, and this magnificent machine was the outcome – A Merryweather 'Metropolitan' Pattern Steamer which could produce 350-400 gallons per minute.

The steam engine, which provided the power to pump the water, was kept in a state of readiness, the water in the boiler being kept heated. The two horses may have been stabled near the fire-engine station, but it is known that at times the Co-op bread-van horses were pressed into service.

The fire alarm was given by the tolling of a single bell in the Town Hall steeple. Local urchins quickly found the location of the fire and great cheers went up from them when the galloping horses, pulling the engine belching smoke and sparks, arrived. The horses were unhitched and the conflagration promptly dealt with, much to the relief of Mr. Dickinson, who was not only Superintendent of the station, but also the Borough Surveyor.

The helmets were supplied with the engine, and had "crossed axes and hose" badges on the front.

The wood yard in Tweedmouth was the biggest fire risk in the area, and before the purchase of the steam fire engine, it would have been impossible to control a fire there with the existing hand pumps.

The top photograph shows the Town Hall clock with a solid black face, which dates the photograph to before 1887 (prob c. 1880), as an illuminated transparent dial was installed after 1887 to commemorate Queen Victoria's Golden Jubilee.

The shop on the extreme left is P & J Cowe's, fish and game dealers, but further down a lady is standing at Crawford's Alley, keeping an eye on her fish stall on the street – probably one of the Bostons, who did have a stance there for selling fish. On the extreme right at the corner of West Street is J. Dunlop & Son, Linen Drapers, whose shop windows have folded brass windowsills, which would be polished every working day by the apprentice.

25 years later in the other photograph, the town hall clock now has an illuminated white dial and J. Dunlop & Son have moved to a prominent site on the other side of the High Street.

In front of the Town Hall steps there is a shelter for the Hansom cab drivers, while on the left of the street is a Brougham 4 wheeled cab standing outside Wood's Temperance Hotel, which occupies the site of what was P & J Cowe's shop.

On the right hand side was Thos H Lawson, hatter at 51, and Samuel Oliphant, manufacturing confectioner at 45 and 47, whose sign proclaimed their Berwick Cockles as being the best. At the top of Hide Hill was a tobacconist James E Ainslie.

C 1900. A small flock of sheep is being driven up the Marygate by a man and collie. Two horse-drawn carts and one carriage and less than 20 people occupy this spacious looking Marygate in about 1900.

The lower picture is of Berwick's original stocks, shown in their old position, at the side of the Town Hall steps. These were last used in 1849 when Grace Guthrie was confined in them for 4 hours for drunkenness and not paying the 5/- (25p) fine. Another miscreant was Bess Knox, who sat with her apron over her head, but who was released early because she was telling so much about the towns' notables!

The carved masonry on the bottom step of the Town Hall came from the previous Guild Hall, which had become dangerously ruinous by 1749. A Guild Hall has been on this site since the middle of the 13th century. In the background a horse-drawn baker's van stands with its door ajar showing a variety of loaves which had names like Turog, Veda and Bermoline.

There are at least two, if not three Rolls Royces shown in the interior garage photograph, the original of which is titled "Berwick, early 20th century". Date probably pre 1914 and thought to be Ford's Motor Car Garage, situated at that time in the Kings Arms Hotel yard.

Subsequently, around 1925, Fords Garage moved to premises in the Red Lion Hotel in the Marygate. This famous 18th century hotel was where the Royal Mail coaches and the Union stagecoach stopped for half an hour for supper or dinner on their journeys to and from Newcastle and London.

The Border Wheelers Cycling Club members are shown outside the Lion Garage prior to a run to Bamburgh in June 1933.
    Shortly after this photograph was taken the Red Lion was no more, having been demolished to make way for Woolworths Store, which moved from its Hide Hill premises.

The photo with the children clustered in the foreground (some with bare feet) c. 1905, shows the Maclagan statue on its original site, before it was removed in 1922 to a site near Berwick Infirmary. Dr Maclagan was a much-loved local doctor.

The other photograph, taken a few years later, shows Skelly the butcher's shop on the corner of Walkergate and Marygate. A horse and cart belonging to Johnson and Darling, brewers, of Governors' Yard, heads up through the Scotsgate. Johnson and Darling were very proud of their Guisachan Scotch Whisky, and surprisingly one unopened bottle of this whisky still exists in private hands today.

About 40 years separates these two photographs taken from the same viewpoint. The older one with a deserted Marygate (and a black dial on the Town Hall clock) shows clearly the unbroken line of fine buildings on the south side, long before the Royal Border Bridge access was brought through Golden Square.

In the 1920's picture, cars are parked on the south side, and groups of men are congregated on the road outside the shops on the north side. This would appear to show the mid-summer hirings in progress, when, if an agricultural worker had been successfully contracted a celebratory high tea for him and his family might follow. This was often taken in Cairn's tearooms or on the other side of the Marygate, the Welcome bakery and café.

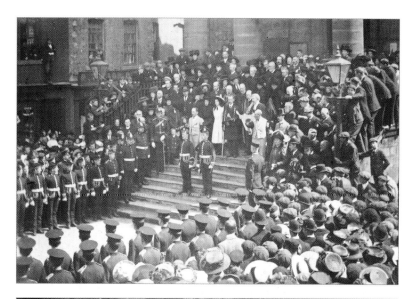

On 9th May, 1910, a proclamation of the accession to the throne by George V was read by the Town Clerk on the steps of the Town Hall.

This was three days after the death of Edward VII, and as a mark of respect, the Mace Sergeant's halberds were draped in black.

After the proclamation, a long procession made its way to the Parish Church for a memorial service. Large crowds watched as the mayoral party crossed the Parade, attended by troops, police and Berwick organisations including the Boys Brigade. The Mayor's Mace Sergeant, Mr. W S Blakey (1926) is standing in the Mayor's parlor with his ceremonial halberd dating from 1685 when Ferdinando Forster was Mayor.

c.1907 The Woolmarket, looking north when it would appear the bins had just been emptied. Formerly called Crossgate, i.e. the street leading to the Market Cross, which stood where the Town Hall now stands.

The buildings on the left have all disappeared, including the Sun Inn (licensee Alex Virtue) at 36. Further down at 28 was the Unionist Club (headquarters Conservative Party) with the Union Jack flying proudly from a very tall flagpole.

The opening of the Unionist Club took place on the 3rd May 1900. David Herriott of Sanson Seal hands over the key, surrounded by bowler and top hatted men. One cloth-capped man is half-hidden by the strange faceless man on the right whose face has been blotted out – did he perhaps subsequently defect to the Liberals? On the other side, near the distant lamppost is No. 35 The Anchorage, recently restored to its former glory by Mr and Mrs Shiel Dodds. This was the home of Dr Johnston, the famous natural historian who was the founder of the Berwickshire Naturalists Club.

In the older photograph the building in the centre was the Peacock Inn, where the HBOS bank now stands. On the left was the Black Bull Inn, where Oliver Cromwell was reputed to have lodged in 1650. Carriers carts belonging to Mr William Fish are loaded and ready to leave for Bowsden, Howtel, Lowick and Milfield.

In the other photograph (c1953) part of a large seagoing vessel, built by the Berwick Shipyard is being squeezed round on to Hide Hill from Bridge Street by a Pickford's Heavy Haulage truck.

Behind can be seen the signs of the British Linen Bank and Savings Bank, which speak of an era before banks become too big and voracious.

The Sandgate has seen
many changes, with the
former Corn Exchange
on the right (built 1858)
firstly being transformed
into a swimming pool
and subsequently into
modern flats. The
Exchange was one of
the most important in
England in terms of trade
and on busy days, Scottish
farmers would refresh
themselves in a pub on
one side of the Sandgate
while their English
counterparts would be
in the pub on the other
side..

Hide Hill with its steep slope was deliberately not cobbled
like the other streets in Berwick, so that horses' hooves
could get a grip on a yielding surface. A hansom cab and
a small dogcart are abreast going up the hill, and in front
of Carrs King's Arms Hotel is a fully loaded coach and
horses, with people sitting on the top outside.

On the left of the street Mrs C.L. Davis has a projecting
sign advertising her circulating library.

In Dewars Lane off Bridge Street is an 18th century granary, with massive walls and a lean more severe than the famous leaning tower of Pisa. Two workmen are loading sacks of grain on to the cart via a wooden slope.

This granary has recently been wonderfully restored and now houses extensive Youth Hostel accommodation, an Art Gallery and also a restaurant.

Another alley off Bridge Street is the Sallyport and the arch at the far end gave access to the area in front of the Town Walls so that troops could quickly respond to an attacking force.

The Old Hen and Chickens Inn (licensee D Fairbairn) on the left, has now been replaced by an Indian Restaurant, The Magna Tandoori. Another Hen & Chickens Inn in the Sandgate is at present empty and for sale.

Two pictures of Bridge Street, taken by Joseph Hunt Thompson, whose father Ralph owned the bakery business shown here which was established in 1835. Joseph, writing in the early 1900's, gives an account of the digging of foundations for a house at the foot of East Street.
– *"The remains of a rude pier were visible with iron rings attached to the stones for the purpose of mooring vessels"*.

The Scotch Ovens belonging to the bakery, still exist in the garden behind the shop, where the ground rises steeply to the line of the ancient defensive Cat Well Wall (c 1562).

Other old ovens still in situ exist below ground level at a solicitor's office further along Bridge Street, and in Love Lane are cellars with foundations which are probably part of the Ravensdale Priory, with its origins going back to the 13th century.

Undoubtedly, centuries ago, the level of Bridge Street was much lower than today, and it remains probably the most interesting street in Berwick.

A glimpse of a pre 1869 Berwick shows a medieval building with crow- stepped gables at the end of the Old Bridge. This stood on the site of a 13th century hospital, the Maison Dieu.

A Victorian building with balcony and crow-stepped gables now stands on the site, and forms the backdrop for a placid scene of an Edwardian lady with straw hat and parasol.

The other photograph from 1956 is anything but placid, for it shows a newly built tug being manoeuvred with inches to spare, on its way from the Berwick Shipyard to the King George V dock in London.

Bankhill 1882. The sapling trees have been planted, almost masking the icehouse halfway up the slope. At the top is the Corporation Academy (built 1800) and on the right, part of Golden Square, which was demolished in 1924 to make an approach road for the Royal Tweed Bridge.

Looking the other way, two high granaries flank Love Lane, and in the foreground, the roof and walkways down to Spowarts' boathouse, which is also shown in the other photograph with the serried ranks of boats for hire.

Coming from an old Berwick family usually associated with butchering, Robert Skelly was a high-class grocer, and here, his window has been specially dressed for a Berwick Shopping Week. Paynes tea and Pheasant margarine have disappeared from the scene, but Crawfords, Heinz and Fray Bentos are names which still trigger a response. The shop at 31, Church Street, now houses a bible shop.

The Maypole Dairy shop stood where there is now a sports shop, (opposite the south wall of the Town Hall). In contrast to Skelly's window all the produce is labelled Maypole, with best tea at 1/4d (6 1/2p) per lb. Grocers had to serve a 5 year apprenticeship and were expected to be smartly dressed at all times. The hours were long as the shops were open until 8 o'clock at night and 10 pm on Saturday.

The cattle market, long held on Hide Hill on the open street, was moved to Castlegate in 1886, and the photograph shows a busy scene about that time.

The other photograph is of St Mary's Villa in 1887. This was the home of Ralph Dodds, prosperous owner of the old established grocers and provision merchant's business and cafes. His house was decorated in style to celebrate Queen Victoria's Golden Jubilee.

Subsequently the house was transformed into St Ronan's School for boarding and day girls. It then became the Newlands Hotel in the 1920's after which it was the labour and telephone exchange until it, and the Baptist Church, were demolished in 1986 to make way for a supermarket.

c. 1887 Wm. Shiel Dods, the proprietor of The Three Tuns Inn, and the butcher's business at 38 High Street, also had an interest in two farms in the district, so no doubt the meat he sold would be of the finest. This property still stands today and is occupied by a charity shop with a hairdressing salon upstairs.

Twenty years later in 1907, a large gathering celebrated the official opening of the Castlegate premises of Wm. Elder & Sons, Engineers & Iron Founders, originally established in Tweedmouth. Also opened at this time was their Vulcan foundry in the Greenses, and after operating successfully for a century, Wm. Elder & Sons ceased trading.

The building is now owned by a charitable foundation and accommodates offices for small businesses, also meeting rooms.

Strother's Yard, in the shadow of the Town Hall, shows a mixture of houses and artisans' workplaces and undoubtedly dates from the 17th century or earlier. It occupies a site on or near where the Shambles was situated, and probably takes its name from a burgess of Berwick who was Town Clerk in the 17th century. On the right was the Butcher's Arms public house. The licensee in 1806 being a Mrs Pringle.

The other yard, with two workmen having a break, was photographed in 1903 and was titled 'A little bit of Berwick' and was possibly in the area on the other side of the Town Hall i.e. Eastern Lane.

Golden Square in 1924 just before the buildings were demolished to make an approach road for the Royal Tweed Bridge opened in 1928.

Described as a typical Scottish close approached by a pend from Marygate, *'its prevailing atmosphere was gloom and squalor'*. At the far end, on the left, a car stands outside Redfearn's garage, which was originally the Burgher chapel. Today that site is occupied by the Berwick Youth Project, which provides supported accommodation for young people facing difficulties in their lives.

In 1806, Golden Square had a diverse mix of occupations; ranging from two ministers of religion and a schoolmaster, to a dealer in pickled pork, two blacksmiths and a weaver.

The smaller picture shows old buildings on the west side of Palace Green. Known as the Sailors' Barracks, the houses were used as rooms for the old and destitute in the 18th century and were demolished in 1974. In the distance can be seen the tall chimney of the Border Brewery in Silver Street.

When the railway came to Berwick in 1846, the not inconsequential remains of the 12th century castle were demolished. The station as it was originally built, had three turrets and was built to resemble a castle. In this photograph of 1906, the top half of a two-tier tower has been removed, and a chimney stack (complete with a Hudson's Soap advert) has taken its place. At this time the East Coast Railway, co-joined with the Great Northern Railway, operated the North Eastern line.

When the Royal Border Bridge (designed by Robert Stephenson) was opened in 1850, it completed the railway route from London to Edinburgh, and was hailed as an engineering marvel.

The pathway, known as the New Road, which passes under the railway bridge, was built after the Napoleonic Wars to provide local employment. Through the arches can be seen the remains of a strong defensive artillery tower (built 1540) which is linked to the castle by the stepped White Wall.

The Royal Border Bridge with a four carriage local train, the size of the train effectively showing the scale of the massive pillars of the bridge, which is 126 feet above the river.

In the foreground are herring boats laid up for the winter. Some are decked, but the oldest ones are undecked and while they could hold more herring, they were not so safe.

The lower photograph shows farm buildings, trees and cultivated fields, where today a large private housing development (Riverdene) occupies the area.

A Class G5 0-4-4T (67270) stands at Berwick station in the 1950's with fireman McKenzie on the right. This was the St. Boswells train, which provided the transport link for the Borders' holidaymakers who flocked to Spittal, Tweedmouth and Berwick in the Trades Holiday Weeks in the years before the Second World War. Evening trips to Tweedmouth at half a crown (12 1/2p) were also popular. The passenger service was discontinued in 1964.

The other photograph, also taken in the 50's, shows a busy day at Kelso station. The 'Kelsae Trip' to Spittal was an annual event which brought hundreds of children to the seaside on a days outing. All the other Border towns had similar outings, usually associated with church Sunday schools.

After arriving at Tweedmouth station the children would process past the engine sheds and down the Billendean with banners held aloft. After the delights of sand and sea, tea was provided along with a paper bag containing dry buns.

The Berwick Amateur
Rowing Club's Annual
Regatta (c. 1900)
when the races were
rowed from and to the
boathouse, as far up
the river as New Water
Haugh. As can be seen,
the viewing area was
extremely congested, not
to say dangerous, and
today, regattas are held up
river at West Ord and in
June, not on the August
Bank holiday as formerly.

The other view shows
four elegantly dressed
Edwardian ladies,
one sporting the club
insignia on her blouse.
Above, on the balcony
of the clubhouse, four
gentlemen, perhaps their
beaus or husbands, keep
a watchful eye on the
proceedings.

Ferryboats at the Berwick side awaiting passengers c.1902. In one, a breezy day causes two ladies to hold on to their hats while alighting.

The period between 1294 and 1376, when there was no bridge, meant that ferries were the only means of crossing to Berwick, and in 1310 six crossbowmen were paid "to guard the ferry of the Tweed at Berwick". In the 19th century and into the first years of the 20th century, even when the iron¬clad paddle steamer 'Susan' was ferrying passengers, individual ferrymen still plied their trade.

The other picture shows a Fifie drifter (herring fishing boat), being oared up river with help from the sail, while four ferrymen sit on the prows of their cobles awaiting customers.

The Shoregate, built in the 1760's, allows access to the Quay and has its original wooden doors. Through the archway can be seen the Corn Exchange, also a broken down cart, no doubt waiting for the cart breakdown service! In places between this gate and Berwick Bridge, parts of the medieval wall can be inspected.

The Pier Gate was built in 1815 to allow passage between the town and the new pier and lighthouse, shown nicely framed in the opening.

The Cowport, the only original gate in the Elizabethan Walls, with its massive doors was built in 1595, and gets its name from the medieval Cowgate through which the townspeoples' cattle were driven to the fields. Just beyond the Edwardian lady standing in the shadow, is the slot where the portcullis dropped down. The roadway at this time is roughly cobbled, and the masonry is showing signs of deterioration.

The Scotsgate as it stands today replaced the original smaller opening in the walls some 200 years ago. In 1745 there would have been a drawbridge over the moat at this gate, and this would have had to be lowered to allow General Sir John Cope entry to the town after his defeat at Prestonpans by Bonnie Prince Charlie.

c.1904, 13.55 hours on a hot mid-summer day, and a troop of soldiers are paraded on the barracks square. In the shadows of the gate, a small barefooted boy looks on, innocent and unknowing of the possibility that in ten years time, he could well be a participant or a casualty in the bloodiest of wars.

The K.O.S.B. sergeant at the Cow Port has his hands in his pockets and is obviously 'at ease', but he would probably have put a soldier of lesser rank on a charge 'for being improperly dressed' if his top pockets had been unbuttoned as his are.

This picture of the Magdalene Fields probably shows the 7th Northumberland Fusiliers on their first camp to Berwick in 1909. The tents are in ranks and a kit inspection seems to be on going. On the left smoke issues from the cookhouse stoves and in the foreground three gentlemen golfers are playing on the carefully marked-off green, while a lady with a pram is an interested bystander.

On the Parade, about the same time, soldiers of the K.O.S.B are being drilled while the rest of the squad, belts and bayonet sheaths blancoed white, stand at ease awaiting their turn to be shouted at by the sergeant.

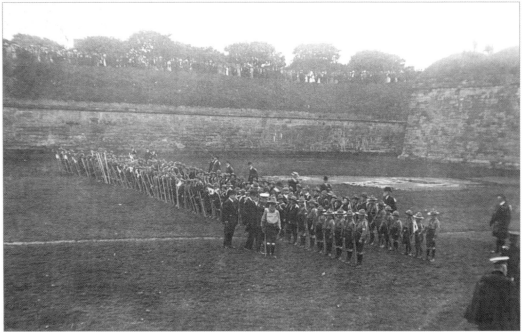

The Traverse or Covered Way, was an earthwork built between 1564 and 1565 to close off the vulnerable Magdalene Fields to the east of the town, thus improving Berwick's system of defence against the Scots.

The spire of Wallace Green church can be seen in the distance, also the roof of the Parish Church.

The Stanks nearby provide the setting for an inspection of Boy Scouts by Sir Robert Baden Powell (c.1910). This occasion has attracted a large number of spectators on the walls, no doubt drawn by the chance of seeing the hero of the Mafeking siege (some 10 years earlier). Baden Powell founded the Boy Scouts movement in 1908, and was raised to the peerage in 1929.

Entrance to the Brass Bastion (built 1563/64) and Flanker interior (with iron cannon balls weighing 1cwt each)

Shortly prior to these photographs being taken (1909) a Committee for Berwick's Historic Monuments had been formed to preserve the walls for posterity. Thanks to citizens like the Vicar of St Mary's Church, (Rev. James King), and Berwick's benefactor, Commander Norman R.N. , steps were taken to prevent the Town Council demolishing more sections of Edward's Wall (dating from c.1300) – the Council's motive being "in order that the site, thus enhanced in money value (would be) for the benefit of the 'Freemen' of the town."

The committee also engaged workmen to clear accumulated earth and rubbish in the flankers of the Elizabethan Walls and do restorative work, so that their noble efforts were eventually recognised by the Crown, and the walls were placed under the care of H.M. Ministry of Works – now English Heritage.

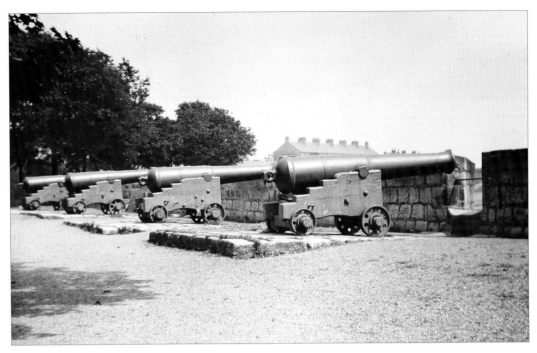

Fisher's Fort, an artillery battery with six emplacements, had, until the Second World War, these English naval guns (32 pounders), some of which are now displayed on the barrack's square. Now only one cannon remains – a Russian cannon captured in the Crimea.

The view of the walls from the estuary shows an industrial chimney and a malting's ventilator, these being part of the Tweed Brewery which was sited in the Governor's House gardens in Palace Green and which was owned by Johnson and Darling.

On the Tweedmouth side of the river, can be seen Shorts Grain Mill, a large building destroyed by fire in the 1920's

Dating from 1297, the White Wall descends *"with Cyclopean steps"* as the Revd. James King puts it in his booklet of 1906. Running down to the river from Berwick's Castle, it terminates in the Water Tower, a defensive feature with guns able to rake the lower reaches of the river and also serving as a landing point for friendly forces.

It has been recorded that a massive chain was stretched across the river at this point to prevent enemy ships infiltrating up river.

In the square picture, an "Edwardian" lady and gentleman adopt a precarious pose, next to the original "Edwardian's" White Wall.

The view (c.1905) looking through a gap in the White Wall shows Tommy the Miller's field, with a Victorian house situated on the recently urbanised Castle Terrace. Near this house, a gallows was established in the 14th century, and this site was where the poor unfortunate Grace Griffen was hanged in 1823 – the last woman to be hanged in Berwick. Most history books about Berwick are remarkably reticent about this shameful chapter in the Town's history, and it may be that some burghers had good reason to want her voice silenced.

The other photo shows the beautiful ashlar facing stone of the castle, contrasting strongly with its inner random core. Most of this fine hewed stone was robbed for buildings in the town, including the Parish Church and the barracks.

Not a trace remains today of these Soldiers' Married Quarters, which were situated above the Blackwatch Tower near the Nessgate. Only the base of this tower remains, and originally it would have been twice this height.

The Bell Tower, situated on the line of the medieval wall, which protected Berwick from the 13th to the 16th century, was originally built in 1392 with subsequent rebuilds. It acted as an alarm tower for any possible invasions by land or sea. As can be seen from the smaller picture, inset, it was also used by the Greenses' fishermen and families, and this is thought to be their Easter picnic, when eggs would be rolled down the grassy banks, and men would display their daring by standing on the rim of the tower.

The bearded gentleman wearing a cape was David Allan, aged 95 who as a youth of 17 had been present at the opening of the Royal Border Railway Bridge in 1850. He is seen shaking hands with Mrs Mabel Philipson, Berwick's M.P. from 1923 - 1929, on the occasion of the opening of the Royal Tweed Bridge in 1928. Mabel was formerly a leading musical comedy actress who took a principal role in the original production of *"The Merry Widow"* in London.

The third member of the group (with bowler hat) was David Allan's nephew, Joseph H Thompson, the gentleman who, as an extremely gifted amateur photographer, was the originator of a large number of the photographs presented in this book. Joseph Thompson's Father was Ralph Thompson who established a bakery and confectionery business at 26 Bridge Street in 1835, which continued until the late 1930's.

Facing page: c. 1878 Berwick's 400 year old bridge was according to Cobbett *"the pass of all these pestiferous feelosofers* sic (Philosophers) *who have done so much mischief to their own country, as well as mine"*. Most of the philosophers he was referring to were Scottish, including Adam Smith and David Hume, and undoubtedly he was not the only Englishman who resented the influx of "Scots on the make" who passed into England over the bridge at Berwick. Hearts were broken on the old bridge too, for John Gray Henderson, of Abbotsrule near Hawick, who became a surgeon in the East India Co, parted from his father on the bridge in 1778, never to meet again. The wall to the right of the horse and cart shows signs of knife sharpening. The copingstone has been splashed with water and its height reduced after years of being used as a whetstone.

The other photograph shows the earliest beginnings of the Royal Tweed Bridge in June 1925 showing cranes, cantilever pile drivers and a mobile steam power engine. The first caisson is under construction and piles of timber struts lie on the shore. At times timber would be carried away by river floods and retrieved from Scremerston beach two days later.

Two rare photographs, showing the smithy in the West End, Tweedmouth, which was demolished when the Royal Tweed Bridge was built.

Cartwheels stand outside the smithy on the right, while on the left two old ladies are chatting at the door of Wm. Hartley's fish and chip shop.

The blacksmiths shop was owned by Wm Taylor, and remarkably two blacksmiths have been photographed in the interior, with its contrasty lighting, one gripping a horseshoe in his pincers. This was the smithy where the chisels were tempered and sharpened for the stonemasons who built the old bridge 400 years ago.

Dwarfing the houses and Tweedmouth Church steeple, this iron hulled barque the *Ardvar* was built at Duncan's shipyard in Port Glasgow, and sailed on her maiden voyage to Auckland, New Zealand on 25th October 1875. She arrived at her destination on 16th February, 1876, almost four months after her departure. Her length was 197 feet with a beam of 32 feet and a registered tonnage of 858 tons. Her fore and main masts were square rigged, and her mizzenmast, fore and aft rigged. This photograph, taken about 1906, shows Tweedmouth railway sheds (back left) and a herring drifter, tiny in comparison to the *Ardvar*.

The other photo shows the dock with a two masted schooner on the left and a three masted wooden hulled barque. The Harrow Inn is prominent (centre left) also Tweedmouth farm with its chimney.

The older photograph, (c.1907) shows an open field to the east of the 'Tommy' shops (foreground) across to buildings in the West end of Tweedmouth. This open ground subsequently became Osborne Crescent and Road, and the Union Park road in the 1920's.

The term 'Tommy Shops' relates to when these buildings were used as stores and shops by the railway navvies, when the Royal Border Railway Bridge was being constructed. The 'navvies' lived on 'truck' (or tick), receiving tickets for their wages from the bridge contractor, which had to be spent in the contractor's shops. Thus each

pound the navvies earned was worth only fifteen shillings (75p) in the rapacious contractor's shops.

The building with the ecclesiastical window was built for seceders from the Church of Scotland in 1848, and is now the Jehovah's Witnesses Kingdom Hall.

The aerial photograph show how the area was subsequently developed, and how the approach road to the new Royal Tweed Bridge divided the two farms, Town Farm and Home Farm. Numerous haystacks can be seen in the yards on both sides of Prince Edward Road.

During the First World War, the Western Front claimed mens' lives in unbelievable numbers. On the first day of the Somme offensive on July 1st 1916, 21,000 British soldiers died. The year before (1915), the supply of shells to the front began to run short, and munition factories, staffed with female labour, sprang up all over Britain. McBain Brothers, Millwrights, in Tweedmouth was one such firm, and during a War charities Week in Berwick in 1918, they invited the public to come and see the shells being made on Friday, August 30th, 1918 from 2pm - 7.30pm Admission 6d.

The health risks to these women workers shown in the parade, were appalling – filling shells with T.N.T. turned their faces yellow and they became known as 'canaries'

73 days after this event the guns were silenced and the Great War finally came to an end – total War dead 12 million.

Some 15 years later, patriotism was still very much to the fore with this fancy dress parade float in Berwick. Britannia sits on a dais complete with shield and trident, flanked on the right by an Indian rajah and a cowboy (Wm. L Howe). On the left an Empire administrator with pith helmet, and a bush-hatted colonial complete the British Empire tableaux.

Two photographs (c.1914) of old-established public houses in Berwick – the Pilot Inn in the Greenses and The Grove in Tweedmouth.

Ann J. Murphy was the licensee of the Pilot Inn, and she and two other ladies stand at the doorway, while a man (with dog) leans nonchalantly against the lamppost.

The Grove Hotel or Travellers' Rest in Tweedmouth has undergone extensive alterations since James Johnston was the licensee. Four ladies and a girl pose outside the hotel, the older lady on the right being perhaps Mrs Johnston.

The modern photograph shows licensees Michael and Sonia McPhillips standing outside the much-extended Grove just prior to their retiral in 2011.

The distinctive cast iron domed well with trough underneath was situated in Tweedmouth's West End and would serve the needs of a number of houses in that district.

The original photograph is titled 'Meggie Muggies Well' but this may be a corruption of Mugger's Well, a mugger being a travelling person who sold mugs and pots.

The substantial building in the background with shutters for the downstairs windows is thought to be Wm Frederick Herriot's shop at 57 West End.

The other scene dating from the same period (1905) is of the Main Street in Tweedmouth, the houses on the left showing their distinctive white steps which was a common feature up until the second world war, and was achieved by white pipe clay rubbing stones, no doubt manufactured and sold by Tennants clay pipe factory, situated just a stones throw from this scene.

On the right mid distance the Queens Head Public House juts out from Church Road. The tall building on the right and the cottage stand on the site of the Highgate where the tollhouse for the road south was situated.

Workers pose for a photograph, and a box held by one man, makes it clear that this is the smokehouse for Holmes & Sons kippers. The lady on the extreme right was Mamie Barnett, who subsequently became the licensee of the Cannon Inn in Church Street. An enterprising lady she realised that as the number of soldiers at the Barracks was being reduced, there would be too many public houses in the town, so she converted the pub to the Cannon Fish and Chip restaurant, which operated successfully for many years.

The poignant photograph of a fishwife with her shawl and petticoat and creel on her back dates from the 1920's and is thought to be the last of the local fishwives, who advertised their wares by the shout "caller herring" (fresh herring). The author certainly has a recollection of this cry in Spittal in the early 1930's.

A famous fishwife of Spittal was Eppy Boston who in 1897 at the age of 71 was still carrying eight stones of herring in her creel, regularly from Spittal to Berwick. Eppy was married at Mordington Toll when she was 21, her husband's name being Hall. Her grandfather was Robert Boston who started the herring curing business in Spittal.

Working with a steam-operated derrick, men toil on shuttering and concrete pouring, to build the Greenses Haven breakwater. The contractor for this development was Mr MacDonald of Hawick, and the harbour was formally opened in 1897 by the Mayor, Councillor G.A. Harrison. At a total cost of £1000 it was thought it would be greatly beneficial to the local fishermen, and that eventually it might be enlarged and the N.B. railway might run a branch line to the harbour!

The *Berwick Journal* ran a fundraising campaign to help meet the building costs, asking for local residents to donate a shilling (5p) and eventually 3000 shillings were raised (£150).

Fifteen years later the harbour is shown being used for bathing, with a large clinker-built boat laden with children, preparing for a trip round the bay, but no signs of fishing boats.

Tom Brown, the photographer, took this picture of his brother Willie's wedding in 1907. The photographer's one-year-old son (also Tom) sits rather uncomfortably in the baby carriage. The ceremony was conducted in the Parish Church, Berwick, and the group is standing in front of the vestry door. Above the doorway a decorative stone carving taken from Berwick Castle reminds us of the dressed stone robbed from the castle to build the church and the barracks.

Three years earlier in 1904 a Burn family wedding group. The boy with the Eton collar on the right was Tom Burn, whose family firm Alexander Burn & Sons, joiners and undertakers, also operated the seawater baths on Sea Road, Spittal. Another branch of the family ran the agricultural chemists' business at Highgate in Tweedmouth.

Cycling and boating were leisure pursuits for the young ladies and gentlemen of the Edwardian era. Canties, three miles from Berwick on the Whitadder River, was a popular place for recreation in the form of camping and fishing. The boating party photograph shows Canties Bridge as it was before its destruction in the 1948 floods. The Corporation Arms Inn (1831) at the end of the bridge is now a private dwelling.

400 years ago when the riding of Berwick Bounds took place, a horse race was held on the level ground at Canties. Afterwards there was a dinner in the afternoon for those who had completed the circuit, when ribbons were presented for the horses.

The fisher is Ralph Dodds, grocer and provision merchant, who with his son Archie and successors operated the Oriental and New Century cafes in Berwick, as well as cafes in North Berwick, Hawick and Dunbar. Ralph's fishing companion and boatman was Thomas Percy, the coffee roaster for the business. Favourite fishing places were below Horncliffe and Paxton House, where this photograph may have been taken.

The firm of Dodds prided themselves on their freshly roasted coffee beans, done on their premises on a daily basis. Older residents of Berwick still fondly recall the wonderful aroma of coffee roasting – something that is sadly lacking today in the High Street.

A beautifully composed photograph of the Plantation complements the previous river scene. This picture was taken by Tom Brown, and was produced as a postcard in the early 1900's.

Two photographs, featuring the *Susan*, an ironclad paddle steamer which plied as a ferryboat between Spittal and Berwick for more than 60 years.

The *Susan* was built by a Spittal boat builder, Mr Harry Littlejohn, in the 1840's. Its distinctive shape with a stern at each end and a tall smoke stack amidships, meant it could go as fast astern as forward.

Leaving Spittal Jetty c.1900 passengers could see the St Ives herring drifters moored by the beach, also the many chimneys of Spittal indicative of the heavy industry located in the village.

The other photograph of the *Susan* was taken in its semi-retiral years (c.1910), when refurbished and with safety railings, it took as many as 40 passengers at a time on pleasure trips up river to Paxton Woods.

Before the herring quay (south of the Carr Rock) was built in Spittal in 1914, the gutting and packing of herring was done near the foreshore at Sandstell, the herring drifters being moored nearby. Fisher lassies worked at high speed in teams of three, two gutting and one salting and packing. Herring were graded into sizes in the barrels, and the man on the left is banging the top hoop on to a filled barrel, prior to sealing it with a wooden lid.

Before the Carr Rock Pier was built in the 1830's vessels requiring a deeper draught in the port of Berwick, moored at the actual rock itself, which is still visible today as part of the sub-structure of the pier.

Clipper schooners and sailing brigs used the Carr Rock pier as well as some of the sail drifters, one of which is being towed away by a tug. One steam drifter can be seen in this photograph but most steam drifters used the herring quay until the Second World War, after which the herring industry collapsed.

Two public houses in Spittal, one the Albion, still in business, the other, the Ship Inn demolished in 1951.

The Albion Inn photograph (c.1895) shows Thomas Rutter, the licensee with his wife and son. Known as Albion House then, the building today retains the same footprint but the entrance has been removed from the corner to the side on Princes Street, where houses with the typical outside stone stairs are shown.

Andrew and Thomas Wood lived in these houses at this time and both being pilots, would keep watch from the High Banks for Berwick bound ships appearing on the horizon. If a likely ship was spotted, they would row to the port entrance to offer their services.

The Ship Inn, which was clay built, was probably the oldest public house in the Burgh, and was situated on Main Street adjacent to Sandstell Road.

Mr Rutter subsequently took over the Salmon Inn at East Ord, dying there in 1918.

Two views of Spittal, Main Street. The older photograph (c.pre 1885) shows at the south end, a chimney belonging to the Helen Iron Foundry. No tower is visible for St. John's Church, as it was added in 1894. In the foreground is the Spittal Hotel (with bay windows), which was burned down in 1905. To the right of the hotel is a group of three old buildings, at one time the property of Richard Mendham, a carpenter, who became wealthy through smuggling and counterfeiting. Richard was tried and executed in Jedburgh around 1812 in the presence of Sir Walter Scott.

The view from the other end is of an elegant and leisurely scene. The wideness of the street is partly due to the space required for the light railway, which at one time ran from the quarry beyond Huds Head to the jetty, carrying stone for the building of the Berwick Pier and lighthouse.

In 1887 Mr Wm Douglass was the proprietor of the Blenheim Hotel, shown on the left, and this old established business continues today in the ownership of Mr David Bell.

The promenade at Spittal, (c. 1925) showing Forte's original wooden Venetian Cafe, which was later incorporated into the present Venetian Pavilion in 1928. In the far distance, adjacent to Huds Head shiel, is a corrugated iron construction, which was Spittal's Palais-de-Danse, before it mysteriously burned down in 1929. Inset picture shows burnt out smouldering ruin.

The new Forte's Venetian Pavilion had a sprung wooden floor for dancing and a resident orchestra. Its tea dances and evening dances were extremely popular in the 1930's, and with the cachet of being a spa town, Spittal, was indeed one of the North Country's best watering places. After the Second World War, with the rise in motoring and foreign holidays, Spittal became just another venue for a day's outing.

Middle Street in Spittal, (c.1920) shows another aspect, with a low huddle of poor houses, on the left, where today there is a shrubbery and rose garden. Life was not easy for many families at this time, and children running barefoot, not just in the height of summer, was not uncommon.

Both these pictures show Spittal promenade around 1900. The upper picture, probably taken on a Sunday, shows elegant ladies and gentlemen walking near Huds Head. One gentleman is doffing his hat to the passing parade, led by two soldiers of the K.O.S.B. in their walking-out uniform complete with swagger canes. Looking north the number of promenaders is quite astonishing.

The other view shows a workaday aspect, for in the distance, salmon fishers are attracting a crowd of onlookers. The sand on the beach is almost level with the promenade, and show how much the present day beach has been depleted.

Writing a postcard to his mother while he was on holiday in Berwick, a dutiful son penned these lines "25th August, 1920. Last night we went over to Spittal to hear the Pierrots which are just about of the usual class" He goes on "There is one fellow there, who used to be at Portobello and later with Willie's Troup at Peebles" The pierrots also appeared at North Berwick and Dunbar during the summer and like pop stars of today, would have their fans at whichever coastal town they performed at on the East Coast.

The P.C. writer is warm in his praise for Berwick as a holiday resort. "Really this is an ideal holiday, for the weather is absolute perfection. What a pity it was not like this when we were in Peebles"

"Love to all, your dear wee laddie" xxxx

A remarkable life came to a close in November 1917 – that of Henry Demee of Berwick and Spittal, aged 75. For the last 15 years of his life, he plied his ferryboat between Berwick and Spittal, but, starting as a boy deck hand on coastal vessels from his birthplace, Jersey, in the Channel Islands, he was a Bosun, second mate, before finally becoming Ship Master.

His voyages took him to the Barbadoes; New South Wales, Australia (where most of the crew jumped ship to join the gold rush at Ballarat), and Madras, India, where horses and soldiers were being rushed to quell the Indian Mutiny. For a spell, he worked the coastal trade to London for Robertson's Foundry at Tweedmouth (pipes and lamp posts bound for India and the Colonies), before world-spanning voyages claimed him once more.

The photograph is of the Clipper Schooner *Teviot* – 133 tons register built by A. & B. Gowan, Berwick – one of the ships which Henry Demee sailed on.

One of Henry's sons (also Henry) was killed during the Great War in 1915 leaving his widow Sarah to bring up two sons, Harry and Richard, and sadly, the latter was killed in the Second World War in 1943. Sarah Demee, a popular boarding house landlady, conducted her business at 33 Main Street, Spittal for many years.

At the height of the herring season, the sailing herring drifters were packed three and four abreast at the quay, and no time was lost in unloading the "silver darlings".

Most of these boats were known as "Fifies" , a distinctive style of boat with a vertical stern post, but some were made by boat building yards in Berwick, and plied the seas down to Lowestoft along with the boats built in Fife.

As the fishermen haul up the crans, an Eton collared boy, holding fish on a string, looks on, while another two boys on the deck (probably family of the skipper), observe the proceedings.

A steam winch is the only motive power for these boats, and this is used to haul the fish on to the quay, the line being controlled by the fisherman on the left.

Gutting and salting the herring went on as the boat's catches were being unloaded. Since all herring landed had to be salted within a day, the work was concentrated. The newly landed herring were tipped into troughs, (known as farlins), and sprinkled with salt so that the gutters could grip the slippery fish. The packers graded the fish sizes into different barrels and layered them with salt. Finally brine was poured in to the barrels through the bung holes in their sides, after the lid had been rammed home.

Two contrasting photographs, one taken from Berwick's old bridge, and the other taken from the pier looking south.

The latter was taken by Mr. Joseph Thompson, on the 12th July 1912, and shows the "Susan", using its mainsail only, making for port in heavy weather. Considerable strength and skill was needed to handle the sails in rough conditions, especially entering the narrow channel by the lighthouse.

Likewise the skill of the photographer must be recognised in using (by present day standards) primitive equipment to capture a fast moving subject in poor light.

The other photograph shows a tranquil scene. A clipper schooner is moored at the quay with two sailing drifters moored alongside, one of which has oars out over the bulwarks and is undecked – which made it less safe than a decked vessel.

The newly built electric power station can be seen in the background.

This beautiful tranquil scene was captured by Mr Tom
Brown, another gifted Berwick photographer from the
first decade of the 20th century. The centre drifter,
BK1095, was a Coldingham boat owned by Peter Rae. On
the quayside groups of onlookers merge with stacks of
herring barrels, indicating the feverish business of the day
has come to a close.

This photo by Mr Brown, shows a very animated scene with the steam tug *"Flying Cloud"* having just towed the sailing drifters into port, reversing away. The fishermen on the three boats are busying themselves with mooring ropes and fenders, prior to tying up.

The other picture shows the drifters at rest, densely packed along the length of the quayside.

A trio of paddle steamers. The top photograph shows the passenger steamer *Forth* returning to Berwick with a full load of trippers.

The *Forth* operated in the summer seasons in the 1890's and the period before the First World War, taking visitors on excursions to Holy Island, North Sunderland, Farne Islands, Eyemouth and St. Abbs.

The other picture shows the *Forth* moored at the passenger-landing quay, while the Leith tug *'Earl of Windsor'* manoeuvres in mid river at low tide.

In August, early 1900's, a group of Leith registered sailing drifters are making ready and sailing in search of the herring shoals.

The Pier photograph shows the boats making for sea, with their large high peaked lug sail set for a fair wind (the smaller lug sail not being used), while groups of slim Edwardian ladies and gentlemen take the air on the beautifully smooth paved pier.

The carefully posed lifeboat photograph is that of the *John and Janet* (1888 -1903) with its 12 oarsmen (double banked), the coxswain William Burgon, the second coxswain, an oarsman and one other.

The *John and Janet* was replaced in 1903 by the *Matthew Simpson*, and its crew was 10 oarsmen, a 1st and 2nd coxswain and a bowman, and it is this later lifeboat, which is shown in heavy seas, making for the safety of the estuary.

Both lifeboats gave sterling service; the *John and Janet* being launched 25 times saving 34 lives, the *Matthew Simpson* being launched 53 times saving 60 lives, before it was taken out of service in 1924.

It has been largely forgotten, but the harvesting of wild salmon from the River Tweed from the 12th century onwards, was the staple trade of Berwick. Other industries grew from this – boat building, and its associated trades, and the quick transport of goods and passengers from Scotland to London by the famous Berwick Smacks, also ships trading all over the globe.

Now, alas, the traditional salmon fishing with net and coble has all but disappeared, after the various stations were bought and closed down by the Atlantic Salmon Conservation Trust in 1987.

Two photographs of salmon fishers at work (c. 1908). One picture shows two ladies in the prow while the men lay the net on the net board, prior to making a sweep out from the beach at Spittal. The other shows a busy scene at Hallowstell, the fishermen with their strong leather boots working intensely, while steamboats ply the estuary.

The tradition of blessing the nets at the start of the season at Pedwell, Norham, was a custom, which lasted until 1986. This photograph shows the Vicar of Norham receiving the first salmon caught after the blessing, on a cold February morning about 7am in the 1940's.

The other photograph shows men pulling in the salmon net at Whitesands which was a lucrative fishing station north of the railway bridge. This fishing was probably part of the Queen's fishing's (Elizabeth I) in the 16th century and Whitesands is its modern name.

This wagon was used as living quarters for workers and would be pulled behind a steam traction engine which belonged to Aaron Oliver of Norham. His business was steam traction ploughing. Another Oliver (Stephen) of Tweedmouth, also had a steam plough based at Beal, while Mary Thew Oliver of Tweed Street, Berwick, had a steam thrashing engine, so at busy times of the season no doubt they would all co-operate.

As shown by the other photograph, steam ploughing entailed two engines pulling a large plough across a field, by means of a cable and huge drums mounted horizontally under the engine boilers. A man using the large steering wheel on the plough (one at each end for reverse operation) would guide the ploughshares across the terrain.

Footnote: One worker has a violin, the other a melodeon, while the third, on the steps of the wagon, carries food on a plate. On the ledge is a Robertson Sandersons Celebrated Mountain Dew Whisky Bottle, so obviously their lives were not all work and no play.

Two corn mills. The older photo is of Twizel, c.1870, where workers dressed in their whites, load sacks on to a cart, possibly for delivery to a flour merchant in Berwick.

Twizel, meaning storehouse, is of ancient origin, for "Agnes de Twsel" of the county of Berewyk" rendered homage in 1296 and had her lands restored to her.

Horncliffe Mill lies in "one of the prettiest little valleys in the North of England". Visitors to the Berwick area were always recommended to visit Horncliffe Glen "famed for its old mill and picturesque scenery", and the two gentlemen, one with a straw boater, and holding a camera in his lap, have obviously taken this advice and will be hoping for a memorable photograph.

The Union Chain Bridge, crossing the River Tweed near Horncliffe, was erected in 1820, and it was Europe's first suspension bridge carrying road traffic. On the 26th July, 1820, 600 spectators crossed the bridge after it was formally declared open, and some three years later, the famous engineers, Father and Son Brunel, came to study this technological marvel, connecting Scotland and England as it did and replacing a hazardous ford.

The toll-keeper's house built into the tower and cliff on the English side was demolished in 1955, and here it has been photographed on washing day, in the early 1920's. Mrs Roxburgh is on her hands and knees, scrubbing her doorstep.

Two rooms, one on each side of the door, housed Mrs Roxburgh's family of five. A well and outside closet were positioned to the left of the house.

The general view shows the graceful lines and record-breaking span of 449 feet – the carriageway, wide enough "to allow two carriages to pass betwixt the footpaths".

Lamberton Toll is shown here in 1890 with a horse and trap and a penny-farthing cycle, also in 1920 with a bull-nosed, two door Morris Oxford. Lamberton Toll was renowned for irregular marriages i.e. marriages not performed by a priest. Couples under age, or of the Presbyterian faith (who were not allowed marriage in a church in England) could cross the Border, go through a ceremony and receive a certificate stating they were married.

The third picture is of Paxton Toll. The tollhouse is out of the picture on the right, but on the left is the track to Yardford on the River Tweed, this being a section of the Bound Road.

Possibly even pre-Roman, this track is part of a road called the Devil's Causeway, which comes from Corbridge, south of Hadrian's Wall. Shown in a map of 1769 it crosses the Tweed and the Whitadder and marches in a straight line to Mordington and Scotland.

Two contrasting buildings at Mordington, on the border between Scotland and England on the Duns road.

The Georgian Mansion was demolished in 1973. The previous building hosted Cromwell in 1648 and 1650 prior to his Scottish campaigns, while he waited for men and supplies to be shipped into Berwick.

The other building (which housed a Post Office and shop), also demolished, was part of the Starch House Toll, named after a starch factory, which was sited here.

Starch made from diverse sources such as potatoes, corn and wheat, was used in laundering, but was also used in papermaking, which was an important trade in Berwickshire from the 18th century.

The tollhouse keeper at Mordington married eloping couples, as at Lamberton, and as there was an alehouse adjoining there was an opportunity "for persons of low character from Berwick, to buy spirits there and convey them secretly into England".

Two views of Paxton c. 1906. In the statistical account of 1841, Paxton's scholars at the village school were listed as being taught – Reading; Grammar; Latin; Arithmetic; Geometry and Writing. The parish school was started in 1619, and it is with some pride that the Revd. John Edgar writes in 1841 that "with two or three exceptions, all the adults in the parish can read and also write".

A traditional Scottish aria, called *Robin Adair*, known from 1739, is associated with Paxton.
One version starts:-
"Paxton's a fine snug place, Robin Adair, It's a wondrous couthie place, Robin Adair"

Another version begins boldly:-
"You're welcome to Paxton, Robin Adair"

In 1814, Beethoven wrote an arrangement for the verses of Robin Adair, but despite being internationally well known, the connection with Paxton remains obscure.

Burnmouth lies at the foot of 100 metre cliffs, 10km. north of Berwick. A map of 1600 (Ponts) shows a mill at the mouth of a burn, hence its name. Perched at the top was a railway station and a junction for the Eyemouth line, which commenced in 1891, both being closed in 1962.

The photo of the harbour shows a road leading south round a high building, and this leads to the hamlet of Ross, a fishing community whose cottages stand close to the high-water mark.

To the north of Burnmouth, a string of cottages at the foot of the cliffs is known by the name of Partanhall, (a partan is Scots for crab), and crab and lobster fishing is still carried on today.

At Burnmouth, the narrow road round the foot of the cliffs is lapped by the sea, and a tiny area below the steep road is occupied by three fishing boats and nets.

The two girls were Maggie Fairbairn and Bessie White, no doubt friends of young Tom who wrote about them on a postcard to his uncle some time in the early 1900's.

The other photograph, taken in "the romantic and sequestered fishing hamlet of Ross" shows a weather-beaten fisherman working on his lines. Typical woven baskets and lobster pots are stacked against the cottage which strangely enough is numbered 13, for fisherman were notoriously superstitious, and 13 would not be looked on with favour.

c.1900 Horse drawn carts at Scremerston being loaded with coal from the railway wagons on the siding, while the newest innovation, a steam lorry, trundles past the Deputy Row houses.

Coal was mined here from the 16th century until 1959 when it ceased, due to falling demand and water inundation.

The quality of the coal produced was not high, and it is known that the captains of the paddle steamers, *Manchester* and *Rapid*, belonging to the Berwick Shipping Co., preferred not to coal their ships with Scremerston coal.

The other photograph shows Scremerston Railway Station, which was one mile from the village, with wagons and carts waiting for the crossing gates to be opened.

In the 11th, 12th and 13th centuries, churches in the Scottish and English Borders had need of defensive features.

In the west end of the Ancroft church (top photo) a very visible pele tower can be seen, and while Doddington church has no defensive tower visible, it is thought the lower stages of a former tower were discernible when disruptive alterations were done in the 19th century.

All villages in the area were subjected to severe depredation by Wallace's raids of 1297 "when the manors were burnt and destroyed"

Constant warring over the centuries led to the building in Doddington of a Bastle house in 1584, which is extant today. Now Doddington is more famous for its deservedly popular local cheeses and ice-cream.

Bondagers singling turnips at Scremerston.

The word bondager sounds rather sinister and may wrongly be thought to imply serfdom or slavery. It comes from the time when farm servants were engaged for work by farmers on "Hiring Days" which took place in the Spring and Autumn.

When a male farm servant was engaged, if he could promise either a daughter or his wife as extra workers, a better job or house could be his reward. In country districts, bondagers were greatly respected, and their distinctive way of dressing made them instantly recognisable. They wore straw bonnets with a scarf tied round the heads to preserve their complexion, with blouses, kerchiefs and thick skirts completing their ensemble.

A rural scene at Bowsden or, as part of an old rhyme has it, Bowisdon.
"Of a' the towns e'er I saw Doddington for rye; -
Doddington for rye, Bowisdon for rigs,
Of a' the towns e'er I saw Barmoor for whigs; -"

Rigs is thought to mean having fun or playing tricks
Whigs – the Liberal political party.

The Plough Hotel at Beal on the A1, sited near the N.E. railway station, was run as a family and commercial hotel by Aaron D Morton when this photograph was taken in the early 1900's.

Shortly afterwards it was taken over by the People's Refreshment House Association (chairman: Bishop of Chester).

The aim of this association was to promote respectable refreshment houses, with less emphasis on alcohol, although it was available. To remove the temptation to the manager to push the sale of intoxicants, he was paid a fixed salary, which could be enhanced however by a share of the profits from tea, coffee, temperance drinks and food served promptly, and of the highest quality.

These hotels became quite popular in mining towns in Scotland, and throughout England, especially in agricultural areas.

In 2007 The Plough (now in private hands) was completely refurbished and re-named The Lindisfarne Inn.

Another Plough Inn was this one at Shoreswood, whose licensee was E. Robertson, and which is no longer extant.

A McLaren compound 828 traction engine owned originally by Thomas H Murdy, Thornton Mains, and bought new by him in 1905, was the inadvertent cause of his death. A month or two after the purchase, a wagon being towed by the engine south of Berwick, ran over him. He died from terrible injuries after 10 days suffering.

The engine passed to J. & J. Murdy of Beadnell and by 1941 was owned by Robson of Tweedmouth, who occupied a yard opposite Tweedmouth Station.

Working on the roads of Northumberland is this 5 ton steam Foden tipper wagon (Reg. No. X3285) and an Aveling Porter steam road roller c. 1920.

This picture of Wark on Tweed with a traffic-free dirt road and a peaceful aspect, belies its violent history. Here the remains of one of the most important castles on the Border sits on a narrow ridge above the river.

At least thirteen ferocious attacks resulted in the castle regularly changing hands between the Scots and the English.

When Edward III came to the rescue of the besieged Countess of Salisbury, (whose husband owned the castle), he became smitten by her charms. During a ball to celebrate deliverance, a garter of the Countess became detached. Edward picked it up saying "Honi soit qui malypense" (Evil to him who thinks evil), which remains the motto of the Order of the Garter to this day.

Bottom picture: Donaldson's Lodge takes it name from an early 19th century white painted house built for Mr Donaldson, on the south side of the hamlet. It was part of the township of Tillmouth, a medieval village now disappeared, and today, while there are a few more houses than there were in 1914 (25), no shops remain.

In medieval times, Wooler was in the administrative district of the East March of England.

The frontier between England and Scotland was defined along the Cheviot Hills, which was a considerable barrier to the transporting of troops and cannon, but posed little problem for the reivers.

Wooler provided refuge during troubled times as it had a castle, and a natural defensive position higher than the surrounding countryside.

Today, the attractive scenery in the vicinity makes Wooler a mecca for artists, walkers, fishers and naturalists.

Two views of Seahouses, one showing a girl by a gate post dating from 1910, the other, picturing a very empty main street, is probably post the First World War.

Today traffic in this main street is unremitting, especially at the height of the summer season.

Seahouses is a very popular seaside resort, being the base for trips to the Farne Islands and with sandy beaches, plenty accommodation and numerous restaurants and cafes, it offers all the holiday maker requires.

Commercial sea-fishing is still carried on, as is the traditional smoking of kippers.

Two horses pull a heavy tank wagon, belonging to the Anglo-American Oil Co., oil importers with a branch based at the quayside, Berwick, with James Evans as the agent.

Paraffin oil would be the likely cargo here, for it was extensively used for domestic lighting in the countryside, and also for engines supplying motive power on farms C.1910.

The other photo shows a Model T Ford butcher's van, belonging to L.W. Mole and Sons, butchers, of Seahouses. One lady has already purchased a large joint of beef, while the other customer has her plate at the ready. C1920's

Cycling as a sporting pastime reached its peak in the early 1900's, and this muscular looking racing cyclist is Tom Lilburn.

Lilburn, whose own make of cycle the "Lilburn Path Racer" won 50 1st, 2nd and 3rd prizes and 4 challenge cups in 1909, had his cycle depot at 86 High Street, Berwick, where he also sold gramophones, phonographs, and records.

Later, the business, now in the name of Mrs Emma Lilburn, was recorded in 1914 as being at 106 High Street, and 20 years later, Thomas (his son?) ran the business from 96 High Street.

In the other photograph, three cyclists take a breather at a salmon fishermen's shiel, up river from Berwick. One cyclist sits on the steps up to the fording box, which was used as a lookout tower by the fishermen, to spot salmon coming up river.

Tom. Lilburn.

Soldiers from the barracks are enjoying splashing about in the "gentlemen's pond" at Greenses Haven where, as the Berwick guide book tells us, "Provision is made for either indoor or outdoor dressing"! Also, somewhat enigmatically, "There are no hard and fast regulations as to the freedom with which this pastime can be indulged", and certainly the photographer has captured a lively scene, stopping the motion of the water in mid-air.

To the north of the mens' pool, another pond "is reserved for ladies, where a shelter has been provided for the use of bathers".

The other scene is of the Greenses Haven where children are enjoying a paddle, and fishermens' boats at rest are tied up to the breakwater.

Both pictures are from 1906.

Two studio portraits from Berwick, the first one dated 1904, was used as a Christmas card and shows two little boys sitting very self-consciously in a donkey cart, whip at the ready.

The other photo from the studio of Rokert, 36 West Street, Berwick, shows two young men, cigarettes in their mouths, and caps firmly in position, at the wheel of a mock motor car.

This no doubt was the very latest idea in studio portraits, for at this time (1902) motor cars were still, in the words of a titled Border gentleman, "an uncertain means of locomotion and in the case of my having an important engagement to keep, I should prefer to trust to horses".

When the famous American midget Charles Stratton, known as General Tom Thumb came on a final tour of England in the early 1870's, he had been married to his diminutive bride for 8 years.

This photograph shows them on their wedding day. Lavinia Warren was the bride and was the same height as the General, who was 2 feet 5 inches when he was 13, although when he died aged 45 he had grown another 6 inches.

A connection with Berwick? Yes! His tour of England included Berwick on two occasions, and he was very favourably received by the citizens.

In keeping with Tom Thumb's diminutive stature, the tiny locket shown, has 12 actual photos of the marriage and bridal party, each photograph being half the size of a postage stamp.

The locket is probably a commercial souvenir, sold by the General's publicity people when touring, for it was purchased locally a century after his last visit.

General Tom Thumb was presented to Queen Victoria on two occasions and it was reported that she was captivated by him. Even when her poodle attacked him, and he fought it off with a tiny sword (which was part of his general's ensemble) she "was amused".

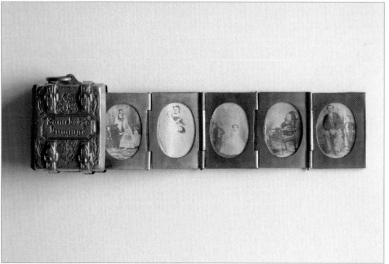

Haggerston Castle. (Top picture). This imposing building was destroyed by fire in 1911, but Christopher John Leyland, the owner, rebuilt the mansion in great opulence, to be described in the *Berwick Advertiser* as "One of the most imposing masterpieces of modern architecture and craftsmanship in the Kingdom".

In 1931 it was demolished and today only the tall tower, with the higher stair turret, stands within a well-appointed holiday complex.

Barmoor Castle, when built in 1801, is supposed to have incorporated an ancient tower house within its walls. For long it was the home of a branch of the famous Sitwell family. In 1911 General Sitwell, a veteran of Gallipoli, pressganged his cousin, the famous writer and art critic, Osbert Sitwell, into a regiment of the Hussars much to Osbert's dismay.

General Sitwell did not always get his own way however, for the 1914/18 war memorial he and his committee had planned for Lowick (four blocks of undressed stone), was rejected outright by the villagers and it now sits in isolation, on the roadside near the castle grounds.

On the 28th August 1907, the 11.22pm braked goods train from Tweedmouth to Newcastle thundered through Goswick Station at high speed, passing signals at red. The train continued its speed until at a connection between the main line and a subsidiary line it veered off the rails. The engine somersaulted over, and finished up in a ditch at the side of the line. The driver and fireman were killed instantly and the guard at the tail end of the train was severely injured, but survived.

Most of the train waggons were wrecked, and this photograph shows about 100 sightseers watching the recovery of the engine by two heavy lifting gear steam cranes.

A photographer busy's himself with his camera on a tripod (on the left) but getting a photograph without including the sightseers would be impossible.

Why did the engine driver go through the red danger signal at high speed? No one will ever know.

Two interesting photographs received just before this book was about to go to press. Both photographs show the sender of the material, Bobby Johnson. Bobby is seen in one, as a small junior choirboy, peeping from behind the robust figure of Bishop Bilborough of Newcastle (with gaiters), who is inspecting the Parish Church Lads Brigade in 1931. The officer at the side of the Bishop is Captain Bob Harvey, and next to the lance corporal on the right, is Joe Booth. Standing in the church porch, half hidden is Mr. White who had the butchers shop in the Marygate.

The other picture shows the Bell Tower School orchestra in 1936. The instrumentalists were from the left:- Olive Ewart; John Henderson; Jean Ritchie; Bobby Fiddes (sadly killed while flying with the R.A.F. in the Second World War); Beatrice Haswell; Bobby Johnson; Mr Gill (music master); Leslie Chappell (obscured), behind Bobby Whillis on the cornet; Alec Hinson; ? Johnston; Mr Dobson; Peter Elliot and Isaac Ritchie.